THE MARVEL OF BEING IN CHRIST

COMPACT EXPOSITORY PULPIT COMMENTARY SERIES

THE MARVEL OF BEING IN CHRIST

Adoring God's Provision of
New Life in the Spirit

DAVID A. HARRELL

© 2020 David A. Harrell

ISBN 978-1-7343452-3-0

Great Writing Publications, 425 Roberts Road, Taylors, SC 29687 www.greatwriting.org

Shepherd's Fire 5245 Highway 41-A Joelton, TN 37080 www.shepherdsfire.com

All Scripture quotations, unless stated otherwise, are taken from the New American Standard Bible® (NASB), Copyright © 1960, 1962, 1963, 1968, 1971, 1972, 1973, 1975, 1977, 1995 by The Lockman Foundation. Used by permission. www.Lockman. org All rights reserved.

No part of this publication may be reproduced, or stored in a retrieval system, or transmitted, in any form or by any means, mechanical, electronic, photocopying, recording or otherwise, without the prior permission of the publishers.

Shepherd's Fire exists to proclaim the unsearchable riches of Christ through mass communications for the teaching ministry of Bible expositor David Harrell, with a special emphasis in encouraging and strengthening pastors and church leaders.

Table of Contents

Books in this Series 6

Introduction 7

1 The Nature of Union with Christ 10

2 The Need for Union with Christ 29

3 The Characteristics of Union with Christ 43

4 The Vine and the Branches 63

Endnotes 90

Books in this Series

Finding Grace in Sorrow: Enduring Trials with the Joy of the Holy Spirit

Finding Strength in Weakness: Drawing Upon the Existing Grace Within

Glorifying God in Your Body: Seeing Ourselves from God's Perspective

God, Evil, and Suffering: Understanding God's Role in Tragedies and Atrocities

God's Gracious Gift of Assurance: Rediscovering the Benefits of Justification by Faith

Our Sin and the Savior: Understanding the Need for Renewing and Sanctifying Grace

The Marvel of Being in Christ: Adoring God's Loving Provision of New Life in the Spirit

The Miracle of Spiritual Sight: Affirming the Transforming Doctrine of Regeneration

Introduction

I count all things to be loss in view of the surpassing value of knowing Christ Jesus my Lord, for whom I have suffered the loss of all things, and count them but rubbish so that I may gain Christ, and may be found in Him, not having a righteousness of my own derived from the Law, but that which is through faith in Christ, the righteousness which comes from God on the basis of faith.
PHILIPPIANS 3:9

There are always times in the life of a believer where the Spirit of God reveals some new insight into a biblical truth that transforms his thinking, redirects his will, and animates his worship to new heights of heartfelt praise. By this I'm not referring to some extrabiblical, private revelation that claims the Holy Spirit speaks to a person directly—the lethal legacy of the Charismatic movement. Nor am I referring to some special illumination whereby the Holy Spirit reveals some hidden meaning beyond the author's original intent in writing a passage that can be immediately understood. This opens the door to false teaching (2 Tim. 2:3-4) and triggers divine judgment (Rev. 22:18-19).

What I'm describing is simply *a more accurate understanding of what the Word has clearly stated*—an enhanced apprehension and appreciation of something profound, but never hidden—something that causes one to say, "Thank you Lord. I was ignorant and confused. I never saw this before, but it was here all along. How exciting!" I experienced this as a young man when the Spirit of God helped me gain new insight into the marvelous doctrine of the *believer's intimate spiritual union with the Lord Jesus Christ.*

I have observed that the vital importance of this sacred mystery remains largely neglected in our current era of evangelical superficiality. As Strong states,

> The majority of printed systems of doctrine . . . contain no chapter or section on Union with Christ, and the majority of Christians much more frequently think of Christ as a Savior outside of them, than as a Savior who dwells within. This comparative neglect of the doctrine is doubtless a reaction from the

exaggerations of a false mysticism. But there is great need of rescuing the doctrine from neglect.[1]

It is my prayer and purpose in this book to help the reader develop a deeper grasp of what it means to be "in Christ," that together we might embrace this intimate oneness more fully by faith and experience more of the confidence, power, and soul-satisfying joy of the presence of our exalted Redeemer. Charles Spurgeon said it best: "There is no joy in this world like union with Christ! The more we can feel it, the happier we are, whatever our circumstances."[2]

1

The Nature of Union with Christ

The glory which You have given Me I have given to them, that they may be one, just as We are one; I in them and You in Me, that they may be perfected in unity, so that the world may know that You sent Me, and loved them, even as You have loved Me.
JOHN 17:21-23

As a teenager growing up in the late 1960s, I was heavily influenced by the "Do this, don't do that" form of Christianity. I was confronted with endless rules and rituals based upon the unique preferences of whatever Christian group I happened to be around at the time (which, of course, varied greatly). I was convinced that only Spirit-filled people lived this way and that they alone possessed His gifts and power; and I truly wanted to join their ranks. So I tried my best to rigidly conform, at least on the outside. But I increasingly felt the sting of an accusing conscience and the shame of hypocrisy when I broke some code of conduct; or maybe kept it, but hated every minute of it. Instead of gaining more power, I felt just the opposite. My legalism only offered an illusion of spirituality. Like many others, I was a lot of sizzle but no steak.

Added to this was the significant influence of older friends I loved and respected who were heavily involved with Campus Crusade for Christ. They taught me the famous "Four Spiritual Laws" written by the founder of Campus Crusade, Bill Bright. Perhaps you know them:

- Spiritual Law #1: God loves you and offers a wonderful plan for your life.
- Spiritual Law #2: Man is sinful and separated from God. Therefore, he cannot know and experience God's love and plan for his life.
- Spiritual Law #3: Jesus Christ is God's only provision for man's sin. Through Him you can know and experience God's love and plan for your life.
- Spiritual Law #4: We must individually receive Jesus Christ as Savior and Lord; then we can

know and experience God's love and plan for our lives.

I still remember a misleading diagram (below) used to illustrate the fourth law. Although I didn't know it at the time, it communicated some erroneous theology that stunted my spiritual growth.

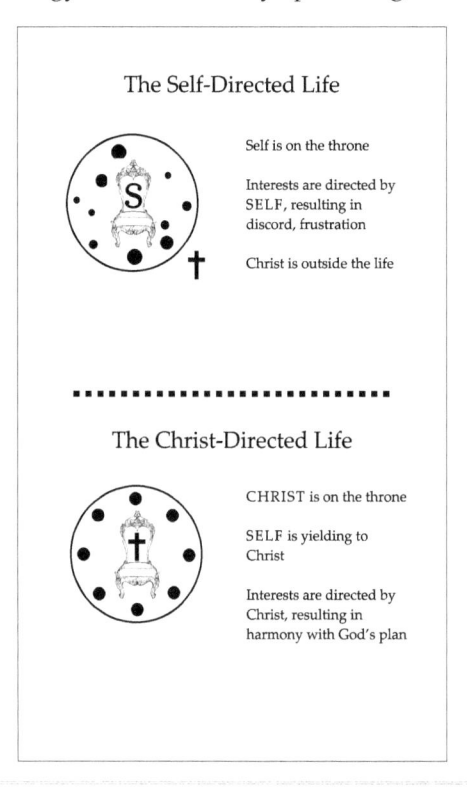

The Self-Directed Life

Self is on the throne

Interests are directed by SELF, resulting in discord, frustration

Christ is outside the life

The Christ-Directed Life

CHRIST is on the throne

SELF is yielding to Christ

Interests are directed by Christ, resulting in harmony with God's plan

Though well meaning, I was unwittingly soliciting Christ to sit on the throne of my life through religious rule-keeping. I wanted Christ in my "circle," not outside of it. I wanted "The Christ-Directed Life" so my "interests [would be] directed by Christ, resulting in harmony with God's plan." I saw myself as the carnal Christian who needed to yield himself more to the Holy Spirit to *gain more filling*, but I was never sure how. Without stating it directly, I secretly wanted to attain more righteousness so God would be more pleased with me—so pleased with me that He would promote me to the status of super-saint. I wanted more Spirit filling so I could have more spiritual power. "After all," I thought, "who wants to be just a run-of-the-mill, mediocre, powerless, fruitless Christian (commonly referred to as a *carnal* Christian) whose interests are out of whack and whose life is not in harmony with God's plan?"

But what I failed to understand is that because of God's gift of grace in saving me, Christ was no longer *outside* me, He was *in* me, and I was *in* Him! Contrary to the diagram, I didn't see myself as a branch attached to the vine that is Christ and therefore, because of Him alone, perfectly capable of bearing fruit (John 15:5). I didn't grasp the astounding reality that the "Father of our Lord Jesus Christ

. . . has blessed us with every spiritual blessing in the heavenly places in Christ" (Eph. 1:3). I didn't understand that I was already "a temple of the living God" (2 Cor. 6:16). I didn't understand "that His divine power has granted to us everything pertaining to life and godliness" (2 Peter 1:3), or that I was to "(strive) according to His power, which mightily works within me" (Col. 1:29) because He alone "is able to do exceeding abundantly beyond all that we ask or think, according to the power that works within us"(Eph. 3:20).

Frankly, I didn't understand the most basic aspect of salvation: *union with Christ*—"that there is . . . no condemnation for those who are in Christ Jesus" (Rom. 8:1); that "if any man is in Christ, *he is* a new creature" (2 Cor. 5:17). I didn't fully comprehend how *His life alone* could satisfy the righteous demands of the Law, *not His plus mine*—consistent with Paul's desire to "be found in Him, not having a righteousness of my own derived from *the* Law, but that which is through faith in Christ, the righteousness which *comes* from God on the basis of faith" (Phil. 3:9).

I simply did not realize that God no longer sees my sin, instead, He sees the righteousness of His beloved Son, "for [I] have died and [my] life is hidden with Christ in God" (Col. 3:3); "For He has clothed me with garments of salvation, He has wrapped me with a robe of righteousness" (Isa. 61:10). Therefore, *I was already in permanent possession of all that is His*.

Baptized by the Spirit into Christ

Sadly, I had such an inflated view of my own righteousness and abilities to impress (manipulate) God that I was unwittingly making a mockery of Paul's words in 1 Corinthians 5:21 where he says, "He made Him who knew no sin *to be* sin on our behalf, so that we might become the righteousness of God in Him." At a most fundamental level, I failed to grasp the miracle of the new birth when I was baptized by the Holy Spirit *into* Christ and what that really meant—which is summarized by the apostle Paul when he said:

> How shall we who died to sin still live in it? Or do you not know that all of us who have been baptized into Christ Jesus have been baptized into His death? Therefore we have been buried with Him through baptism into death, so that as Christ was raised from the dead through the glory of the Father, so we too might walk in newness of life. For if we have become united with Him in the likeness

of His death, certainly we shall also be in the likeness of His resurrection, knowing this, that our old self was crucified with Him, in order that our body of sin might be done away with, so that we would no longer be slaves to sin; for he who has died is freed from sin. (Rom. 6:2-7)

Once I began to realize Christ was not outside of me, separated from me, wanting me to shape up so He could come into my life and really take it over so I could experience the "abundant life" (as my friends called it), everything changed. I was both humbled and relieved to know that *all the righteousness I would ever need to be pleasing to God, and all the Spirit filling I foolishly thought I could acquire was already my permanent possession by grace alone, through faith alone, in Christ alone.* With this, the words of the apostle John took on new meaning to me where he says, "By this we know that we abide in Him and He in us, because He has given us of His Spirit" (1 John 4:13).

Now, it's important to note: *this did not translate into a license to sin.* In fact, just the opposite was true. My heart (like countless others) was animated to pursue godliness like never before as I began to grasp the magnitude of God's gracious gift of *Christ Himself* and as I began to fully realize that I am "complete in Him" (Col. 2:10). Knowing that without Him I can do nothing (John 15:5), I had a passion for holiness for all the right reasons. God was not waiting to be *impressed*, but to be *worshipped*. Christ was no longer a power source to be *earned*, but to be *enjoyed*. I finally understood the heading of Chapter One, Book Three of Calvin's Institutes: "The Benefits of Christ Made Available to Us by the Secret Operation of the Spirit"; there he said,

> We must now see in what way we become possessed of the blessings which God has bestowed on his only begotten Son, not for private use, but to enrich the poor and needy. And the first thing to be attended to is, that so long as we are without Christ and separated from him, nothing which he suffered and died for the salvation of the human race is of the least benefit to us. To communicate to us the blessings which he received from the Father, he must become ours and dwell in us. Accordingly, he is called our Head, and the first-born among many brethren, while, on the other hand, we are said to be engrafted into him and clothed with him, all which he possesses being . . . nothing to us until we become one with him.[3]

Christ Our All-glorious End

As I began to better understand this marvelous mystery—the foundation of all spiritual blessings—my walk with Christ changed dramatically. Rather than seeing *Christ as a means to an end, I realized He was the all-sufficient and all-glorious end Himself.* Christ esteemed this profound reality so highly that it was the primary emphasis in His High Priestly prayer to His Father as He prepared to endure the agonies of the cross on our behalf. He prayed

> that they may all be one; even as You, Father, are in Me and I in You, that they also may be in Us, so that the world may believe that You sent Me. The glory which You have given Me I have given to them, that they may be one, just as We are one; I in them and You in Me, that they may be perfected in unity, so that the world may know that You sent Me, and loved them, even as You have loved Me. (John 17:21-23)

It is impossible to fathom the gulf that exists between our holy Creator and His sinful creatures. For the Son of God to purchase our redemption and be married to such a wretched bride is equally unfathomable. Nevertheless, such was the intended unity decreed before the foundation of the world; and it was this very union between Christ and all whom the Father had given Him that occupied the heart of our Lord on the eve of His crucifixion. That this is recorded in Scripture is certain proof that He wants all who belong to Him to accurately apprehend the nature of this mystical union that we might esteem it as He did. It was His desire for His bridal church to relish the profound implications of this everlasting marriage, that she might enjoy the staggering benefits of what it means to be "in Christ."

This is also at the heart of Paul's doxology recorded in Ephesians 1:3: "Blessed *be* the God and Father of our Lord Jesus Christ, who has blessed us with every spiritual blessing in the heavenly *places* in Christ." That little preposition "in" ("in Christ") signifies the deep wonder of Christ being more than *with* us, more than existing *outside* us, but One who is *in* us, and we are *in* Him. One who is *more* than our sovereign King, our risen Savior, our Lord and Master, teacher or friend, although He is all this and more!

To be "in Christ" is not some mystical form of *pantheism* where Christ is absorbed into the "wholeness" which is God; nor is it a *physical* union (as taught by sacramentarians) where Christ enters men physically by participating in some rite or ceremony; nor is it a union of *essence* where we lose our human identity and become one with God or absorbed into Christ. Rather, it is an expression of interconnectedness whereby we share a common spiritual life with Him, for "[we] have died and [our] life is hidden with Christ in God" (Col. 3:3), he is "our life" (Col. 3:4), and He lives in us (Gal. 2:20).

Scripture reveals some amazing truths about the nature of this union.

- It is a SUPERNATURAL union authored by God: "If anyone loves Me, he will keep My word; and My Father will love him, and We will come to him and make Our abode with him" (John 14:23).
- It is a VITAL union by which Christ becomes our very life: "I have been crucified with Christ; and it is no longer I who live, but Christ lives in me; and the *life* which I now live in the flesh I live by faith in the Son of God, who loved me and gave Himself up for me" (Gal. 2:20; *cf.* Col. 3:3-4).
- It is an ORGANIC union in that with Christ believers form one body (the church) and respond to Christ as the head: "He is . . . the head of the body, the church" (Col. 1:18; *cf.* 1 Cor. 12:4-27; Eph. 4:15; 5:23).
- It is a SPIRITUAL union in that Christ dwells

within us by the Spirit who is the Spirit of Christ (1 Peter 1:11; *cf.* Rom. 8:9; 2 Cor. 3:18); "for by one Spirit we were all baptized into one body . . . and we were all made to drink of one Spirit" (1 Cor. 12:13).
- It is a LEGAL union in that Christ is our representative head who has made us the beneficiary of his substitutionary work of salvation: "So then as through one transgression there resulted condemnation to all men, even so through one act of righteousness there resulted justification of life to all men. For as through the one man's disobedience the many were made sinners, even so through the obedience of the One the many will be made righteous" (Rom. 5:18-19).
- It is a MYSTERIOUS union in that it has no analogy in human experience: "God willed to make known what is the riches of the glory of this mystery among the Gentiles, which is Christ in you, the hope of glory" (Col. 1:27).
- It is an EVERLASTING union that can never be severed: "For I am convinced that neither death, nor life, nor angels, nor principalities, nor things present, nor things to come, nor powers, nor height, nor depth, nor any other created thing, will be able to separate us from

the love of God, which is in Christ Jesus our Lord" (Rom. 8:38-39).

The Holy Spirit helps us grasp this unfathomable mystery by describing it through various figures.

- We are "married" to Christ (Rom. 7:4).
- We are to Christ as a bride is to a bridegroom (Eph. 5:22-23).
- We are branches on the true vine (John 15:1-11).
- We partake of Jesus, the true bread from heaven (John 6:51).
- We are the body and Jesus is the head (Eph. 1:22-23).
- We are a spiritual building "joined together, and [growing] into a holy temple in the Lord" (Eph. 2:21).

The implications of these descriptions are staggering, not only as they relate to the doctrine of salvation, but also how we as believers actually live out this union in our gospel proclamation, worship, service, and relationships with other believers. I stand in awe when I reflect upon the glorious reality that Jesus Christ came to this earth not only to pay the penalty for my sin, but also to establish an intimate, living, eternal union with me whereby I become one with Him. I trust you share my amazement, and my eternal gratitude and joy!

The Benefits of Christ Versus Christ Himself

As I stated earlier, somehow the full, soul-exhilarating reality of this intimate union escaped me in the early years of my Christian life. The primary focus of my initial evangelical training centered upon the *benefits of Christ* in my salvation rather than *Christ Himself*. I would read the gospel narratives and think to myself, "Wow, how can I appropriate these great blessings for myself?" "How must I live my life to tap into what Christ can do for me, because it is only *through* Him that I can be blessed?"

Like many (if not most) Christians today, I thought of Christ in terms of what He *offered* rather than who He *is* and who I am *in* Him. I perceived the gospel offer of salvation as a gift of grace that merely came *through* Christ, rather than *in* Christ. I really didn't see Him as the personification of the gospel; that He *is* the gospel, that none of the benefits of saving grace exist separately from Him, but only *in* Him.

Most of what I heard being preached pertained to the great blessings of Christ and how to secure them for my life, as if they are separate or abstracted from Him. The primary emphasis of my Biblical Counseling training was much more on the practical application of Scripture ("putting off and putting on") than on "[counting] all things to be loss in view of the surpassing value of knowing Christ Jesus my Lord" (Phil 3:8). I became a student of *others* more than of *Christ*; a student of counseling methods more than of Christ; even a student of Scripture more than of Christ who is the wellspring of every spiritual blessing I receive and enjoy! I failed to comprehend what John Murray described as "the central truth of the whole doctrine of salvation."[4]

In many circles today evangelicals are fed a steady diet of many different topics, some good, and some bad. But seldom do they study *the glory and majesty of Christ and what it means to be intimately united to Him*. While we all have our stories, I fear the outcome is the same. In ways that are imperceptible, *Christ becomes a means to an end rather than the all-sufficient, all-glorious end Himself.* A subtle detachment occurs, separating us from the vital and soul-thrilling intimacy available to us through communion with the Lover of our soul—the One in whom we exist, "for we are the temple of the living God" (2 Cor. 6:16). Unwittingly, we walk at a distance from Him rather than closely with Him, leaving us vulnerable to the sin of the Ephesians who, like many believers today, exchanged their love for Christ for a cold orthodoxy that resulted in the forfeiting of divine blessing (Rev. 2:4-5).

We must understand that when the profound reality of our union with Christ is neglected, when we relegate its doctrinal truths to a secondary or tertiary status of consideration, we, too, become strangers to Christ and forfeit blessing in our life. The futility of trying to earn what we already possess in Him not only produces frustration because our service is done in the flesh rather than the Spirit, but it also keeps our focus on *self-effort* rather than *Christ's finished work*. As a result, our worship becomes increasingly *man-centered* instead of *God-centered*, our prayer life becomes little more than a perfunctory and occasional ritual, and our service to Christ lacks both zeal and power. We see this clearly in Jesus' admonition, "I am the vine, you are the branches; he who abides in Me and I in him, he bears much fruit, for apart from Me you can do nothing" (John 15:5).

It is for this reason that we must wholeheartedly embrace this magnificent doctrine intellectually and volitionally, for indeed our union with Christ is "the source of every spiritual blessing we receive—from the Father's election in eternity past, to the Son's redemptive life, death, burial, and resurrection, all the way to the glorification of the saints with Christ in heaven."[5] No wonder Paul told the proud intellectuals in Corinth, "I determined to know nothing among you except Jesus Christ, and Him crucified" (1 Cor. 2:2).

Christ Is the Gospel

Sinclair Ferguson is in agreement with this general analysis as expressed in his summary of how the proclamation of the gospel found in the New Testament, the teaching of the Reformation, and the mainstream Puritans differed from much of what we hear today:

> What was at the heart of their gospel message? Calvin has a beautiful expression that summarizes it: the gospel is Christ "clothed with his gospel." This, to use an Augustinian term, is *totus Christus*, the whole Christ, the person in whom incarnation has been accomplished and in whom atonement, resurrection, ascension, and heavenly reign are now realized.
>
> While we can distinguish Christ's person and his work in analytical theological categories, they are inseparable from each other. Since there is no "work of Christ" that takes

place abstracted from, and in that sense outside of, his person, the blessings of his work cannot be appropriated apart from receiving Christ himself with all his benefits. What God has joined together, we must not put asunder.[6]

This is why it is so important to rediscover—or perhaps discover for the first time—this precious doctrine of the believer's union with the Lord Jesus Christ, our Representative and Substitute, the sacred Mediator of all the blessings of the redeemed. For we have been *crucified* with him (Gal. 2:20), we have *died* with him (Rom. 6:8; Col. 2:20), we have been *buried* with him (Rom. 6:3), we have been *raised* up with him to walk in newness of life (Eph. 2:5-6; Rom. 6:4), and we have been *seated* with Him in the heavenly places (Eph. 2:6).

As together we behold the marvel of being in Christ, we will certainly find ourselves adoring God's provision of new life in the Spirit summarized so comprehensively by John Murray:

> Union with Christ has its source in the election of God the Father before the foundation of the world and has its fruition in the glorification of the sons of God. The perspective of God's people is not narrow; it is broad and it is long.

It is not confined to space and time; it has the expanse of eternity. Its orbit has two foci, one the electing love of God the Father in the counsels of eternity; the other glorification with Christ in the manifestation of his glory. The former has no beginning, the latter has no end. ... Why does the believer entertain the thought of God's determinate counsel with such joy? Why can he have patience in the perplexities and adversities of the present? Why can he have confident assurance with reference to the future and rejoice in hope of the glory of God? It is because he cannot think of past, present, or future apart from union with Christ.[7]

Knowing that we are able to consciously commune with our ever-present Savior who can "sympathize we with our weaknesses" and "who has been tempted in all things as we are, yet without sin" (Heb. 4:15) is a reciprocal expression of love that boggles the mind and delights the soul. With these truths resonating within our heart we can better understand Peter's poignant words when he said, "though you have not seen Him, you love Him, and though you do not see Him now, but believe in Him, you greatly rejoice with joy inexpressible and full of glory" (1 Peter 1:8).

2

The Need for Union with Christ

Although you were formerly alienated and hostile in mind, engaged in evil deeds, yet He has now reconciled you in His fleshly body through death, in order to present you before Him holy and blameless and beyond reproach.
COLOSSIANS 1:21-22

Although Satan will continue to deceive the church by sowing tares among the wheat (Matt. 13:24-30), I fear a failure to underscore man's desperate need to be *united to Christ* in gospel presentations has contributed to this tragic reality. What is needed—and what must be preached from pulpits—is *a sober recognition of the terrifying separation that exists between our Holy God and fallen man that makes union with Christ an indispensible necessity for salvation.* How many professing Christians really understand this? It has been my observation based upon conversations with hundreds of believers over the years that very few comprehend the chasm that has been bridged through their union with Christ. Most don't see themselves as all that sinful, nor do they see God as all that holy; and most don't really understand how Christ fits into the picture, especially as it relates to their union with Him.

Yet we see this explained repeatedly in the New Testament. For example, the apostle Paul reminded the saints in Colossae that before they were saved, they were "alienated and hostile in mind, engaged in evil deeds, yet He has now reconciled you in His fleshly body through death, in order to present you before Him holy and blameless and beyond reproach" (Col. 1:21-22). Likewise, Paul reminded the Gentile saints at Ephesus that before their salvation, they were once alienated, "separate from Christ, excluded from the commonwealth of Israel, and strangers to the covenants of promise, having no hope and without God in the world" (Eph. 2:12). But then, in contrast to this great horror, Paul states the remedy for our estrangement is based upon our union with Christ, saying, "But now *in Christ Jesus* you who formerly were far off have been brought near by the blood of Christ" (Eph. 2:13; emphasis mine).

This state of alienation and hostility toward God is further stated in Ephesians 4 where the unregenerate are described as those who "walk, in the futility of their mind, being darkened in their understanding, excluded from the life of God because of the ignorance that is in them, because of the hardness of their heart" (vv. 17-18). This explains the staggering inability of an unbeliever to understand the spiritual truths in the Bible so as to be saved; every conversation betrays how "a natural man does not accept the things of the Spirit of God, for they are foolishness to him; and he cannot understand them, because they are spiritually appraised" (1 Cor. 2:14).

Controlled by the Flesh

To further underscore our great need to be united to Christ, consider Paul's description of unbelievers being controlled by their flesh: "For those who are according to the flesh set their minds on the things of the flesh, but those who are according to the Spirit, the things of the Spirit" (Rom. 8:5). The life of an unbeliever is dominated by the fallen, sinful nature with which they were born. They live under the authority of their *flesh*: a reference to sinful man's moral inadequacy contained in his unredeemed humanness, his innate inability to conform to the righteous character and desires of God.

What a powerful indictment this is! To "set their minds" upon something is to give continuous and serious consideration to it. It means to ponder, to let one's mind dwell upon, to fix one's attention upon something. It is all they think about. Those who are according to the flesh are bound in their thoughts to the desires of the flesh such as "immorality, impurity, sensuality, idolatry, sorcery, enmities, strife, jealousy, outbursts of anger, disputes, dissensions, factions, envying, drunkenness, carousing, and the things like these, of which I forewarned you just as I have forewarned you that those who practice such things shall not inherit the kingdom of God" (Gal. 5:19-21).

In Ephesians 2 Paul described the pre-conversion marks of our old nature when he said, "And you were dead in your trespasses and sins in which you formerly walked according to the course of this world, according to the prince of the power of the air, of the spirit that is now working in the sons of disobedience. Among them we too all formerly lived in the lusts of our flesh, indulging the desires of the flesh and of the mind, and were by nature children of wrath, even as the rest" (Eph. 2:1-3). Peter also described the unregenerate man as one who seeks to "indulge the flesh in its corrupt desires" (2 Peter 2:10). To the Philippians, Paul wrote, "[They are those] whose end is destruction, whose god is their appetite, and whose glory is in their shame, who set their minds on earthly things" (Phil. 3:19).

It is important to note what Paul did *not* say in Romans 8:5. He did *not* say, "For the mind that is set on the flesh *leads* to death." He said that it "*is* death." What does he mean? He means an unbeliever is alive physically, but he is *dead spiritually*. He is a spiritual cadaver. The unregenerate man lives in the realm of the damned. The wrath of God abides upon him. Because of the offense of his sin against a holy God, he is doomed to eternal death. And that which is dead cannot respond unless God does something! Unless God Himself initiates the restitution, there is none.

Indeed, unless God breathes spiritual life into the sinner, his mind remains set on the flesh. In Romans 8:7 Paul goes on to say, "the mind set on the flesh is hostile toward God; for it does not subject itself to the law of God, for it is not even able to do so." The walking dead love their sin more than they love God. They live for all this world can offer them. They do not subject themselves to the law of God, and are unable to do so. Apart from the regenerating grace of the Holy Spirit that baptizes them *into* Christ, they will remain forever alienated from God. And only the new birth can initiate this union—"But God, being rich in mercy, because of His great love with which He loved us, even when we were dead in our transgressions, made us alive together with Christ" (Eph. 2:4).

The Gospel Offer of Christ Himself

I often find my heart captivated by the magnitude of God's grace in justification by faith alone, despite my sin. Paul expresses this when he says: "[T]here is now no condemnation for those who are *in* Christ Jesus" (Rom. 8:1; emphasis mine). This is a truly astonishing passage of Scripture, allowing us to behold the grandeur and mystery of the gospel of God. Here again we see that the gospel offer of salvation is not a gift of grace that comes *through* Christ; it *is* Christ. He *is* the gospel. None of the benefits of saving grace exist separately from Him, but only *in* Him. For this reason we can rejoice with Paul and say, "Blessed *be* the God and Father of our Lord Jesus Christ, who has blessed us with every spiritual blessing in the heavenly *places* in Christ" (Eph. 1:3).

While this is the only truth that saves (Rom. 1:16), many professing Christians fail to understand it.

According to a Pew Research Center survey, 52 percent of Protestants in the United States say that "both good deeds and faith are needed to get into heaven, a historically Catholic belief."[8] Such lack of clarity on the most basic element of saving grace emphasizes the need for fearless preachers to stand up and "[proclaim] . . . the testimony of God" and, like the apostle Paul, be willing to say to the Corinthians of our day, "I determined to know nothing among you except Jesus Christ, and Him crucified" (1 Cor. 2:1-2).

But this is seldom the case these days. As a result, the glorious gospel offer of *Christ Himself* has been hijacked by clever perversions like the *prosperity gospel* that would have us believe Christ died to make us happy, or the *social justice gospel* that requires the church to advocate for what is fundamentally Marxist Socialism and embrace a cultural definition of justice that is always changing and has nothing to do with the justice of God. Fighting against such distortions (and there are many others), Paul warned, "If anyone preaches to you a gospel contrary to that which we have preached to you, let him be accursed" (Gal. 1:8).

Although many subtle and some not-so-subtle doctrinal aberrations can lead to a false gospel, neglecting the doctrine of a believer's union with

Christ must be among the most dangerous. The pervasive ignorance concerning it and the concomitant apathy towards it prove how it has been disregarded. For this reason, it is important to reacquaint the true church with the same truths the apostle Paul reminded the saints at Ephesus—*that were it not for the union of God's elect in Christ, we would perish in our sins*. Indeed, we would still be "dead in our trespasses and sins . . . [walking] according to the course of this world, according to the prince of the power of the air, of the spirit that is now working in the sons of disobedience. . . . indulging the desires of the flesh and of the mind, and . . . by nature children of wrath, even as the rest" (2:1-3).

This is what makes our union with Christ so glorious. This is what makes the gospel such amazingly good news, because saving grace is more than a gift made available *through* Christ; *it is Christ Himself!* Because we are united to Him we have "peace with God" (Rom. 5:1) which allows us to pass through the veil of separation and have *access to God*. The apostle Paul reveals this astonishing truth when he says that through our Lord Jesus Christ, "we have obtained our introduction by faith into this grace in which we stand" (Rom. 5:2). The writer of Hebrews elaborates on this saying,

> Since therefore, brethren, we have confidence to enter the holy place by the blood of Jesus, by a new and living way which He inaugurated for us through the veil, that is, His flesh, and since we have a great priest over the house of God, let us draw near with a sincere heart in full assurance of faith, having our hearts sprinkled clean from an evil conscience and our bodies washed with pure water. (Heb. 10:19-22)

But these glorious benefits made possible by our union with Christ cannot be fully understood or appreciated unless men or women first come to grips with the horrifying reality of their current condition described in Paul's words to the saints in Ephesus:

> And you were dead in your trespasses and sins, in which you formerly walked according to the course of this world, according to the prince of the power of the air, of the spirit that is now working in the sons of disobedience. Among them we too all formerly lived in the lusts of our flesh, indulging the desires of the flesh and of the mind, and were by nature children of wrath, even as the rest. But God, being rich in mercy, because of His great

love with which He loved us, even when we were dead in our transgressions, made us alive together with Christ (by grace you have been saved), and raised us up with Him, and seated us with Him in the heavenly places in Christ Jesus, so that in the ages to come He might show the surpassing riches of His grace in kindness toward us in Christ Jesus. For by grace you have been saved through faith; and that not of yourselves, it is the gift of God; not as a result of works, so that no one may boast. (Eph. 2:4-7)

Here the apostle elaborates upon our election in eternity past, when, before the foundation of the world, God chose *by* Himself and *for* Himself those He determined to bless "in Christ" (Eph. 1:3), and "predestined [them] to adoption as sons through Jesus Christ to Himself, according to the kind intention of His will, to the praise of the glory of His grace, which He freely bestowed on us *in the Beloved*" (vv. 5-6; emphasis mine).

A Union Decreed in Eternity Past

This is the very heart of the gospel! The grammar in these great descriptive passages in Ephesians clearly indicates that God's everlasting grace that united His elect to Christ was ordained and accomplished in eternity past. In some inscrutable sense, *this is what God has done for us already, not something depending upon us and waiting to happen to us through self-effort.* Although the application of redemption is effectually applied at the moment of regeneration when the Spirit of God raises a sinner from spiritual death to life and implants within him a governing disposition of the soul that is radically *new* and *holy*, He has *already* "made us alive together with Christ" (Eph. 2:5), He has *already* "raised us up with Him, and seated us with Him in the heavenly places in Christ Jesus" (v. 6), "For we are His workmanship, created in Christ Jesus for good works, which God prepared beforehand so that we would walk in them" (v. 10).

What a glorious thought: *though once separated from God by sin, because of His great mercy and love set upon us before the foundation of the world when He chose us in Christ* (Eph. 1:4), He "saved us and called us with a holy calling, not according to our works, but according to His own purpose and grace which was granted us in Christ Jesus from all eternity" (2 Tim. 1:9). In keeping with that union decreed in eternity past, He made us alive with Christ. He effected a union that became the legal basis for the imputation of Christ's righteousness to guilty sinners (since it would be legal fiction for God to say the righteous requirement of the law is fulfilled "in us" unless we are "in Christ"). This is a union so certain that it is described as already accomplished:

> Therefore we have been buried with Him through baptism into death, so that as Christ was raised from the dead through the glory of the Father, so we too might walk in newness of life. For if we have become united with Him in the likeness of His death, certainly we shall also be in the likeness of His resurrection, knowing this, that our old self was crucified with Him, in order that our body of sin might be done away with, so that we would no longer be slaves to sin; for he who has died is freed from sin. Now if we have died with Christ, we believe that we shall also live with Him, knowing that Christ, having been raised from the dead, is never to die again; death no longer is master over Him. For the death that He died, He died to sin once for all; but the life that He lives, He lives to God. Even so consider yourselves to be dead to sin, but alive to God in Christ Jesus.
> (Rom. 6:4-11)

"Holy Affections"

When a man is united to Christ, the indwelling Spirit influences his thoughts through His Word which causes him to be repulsed by the things of the flesh. He will hate his own sin and the sin around him, and in turn will glory in the grace that delivered him from that sin. It is clear that his soul has been awakened to the glory of God, and he will care little for the things of this sin-laden world. He has what Jonathan Edwards called "Holy Affections." The excellency and majesty of Jesus Christ becomes his food and drink and his gaze will remain fixed on the cross. He will not be content with quick glances, but he will dwell upon the One placed upon that cross as his substitute. The cross will become his lifelong study, because it bridged the infinite chasm between his sin and God's holiness. With Isaac Watts he will sing:

When I survey the wondrous cross,
On which the Prince of glory died,
My richest gain I count but loss,
And pour contempt on all my pride.

Forbid it Lord that I should boast,
Save in the death of Christ my God;
All the vain things that charm me most,
I sacrifice them to His blood.

See, from His head, His hands, His feet,
Sorrow and love flow mingled down;
Did e'er such love and sorrow meet,
Or thorns compose so rich a crown?

Were the whole realm of nature mine,
That were a present far too small;
Love so amazing, so divine,
Demands my soul, my life, my all.

3

The Characteristics of Union with Christ

If anyone loves Me, he will keep My word; and My Father will love him, and We will come to him and make Our abode with him.

JOHN 14:23

We've all heard the phrase *truth and time walk hand in hand*, and by experience we know that to be true. What once seemed to be accurate and genuine later proves to be quite the opposite, especially when it comes to a person's profession of faith in Christ. We have all watched in dismay as someone we know proves to be a living contradiction to his profession of love for Christ causing us to say, "I don't think he's truly saved; there's just no spiritual fruit in his life." It is not at all uncommon to hear about some pastor who has abandoned the faith, or who has fallen so deep into doctrinal error or moral failure as to cast legitimate doubt about the genuineness of it. On numerous occasions I have counseled Christian celebrities whose own joyless testimony and personal doubt about their salvation betrays an absence of the indwelling Spirit "who testifies with our spirit that we are children of God" (Rom. 8:16).

Consider the doleful confession revealed in the secret letters of the Roman Catholic nun, Mother Teresa. Ten years following her death, some of her personal correspondence with superiors was published. What the letters unveiled shocked much of the religious world. Famed for her charity work in Calcutta, India, Teresa admitted that she spent almost fifty years of her life without sensing the presence of God. She bemoaned a spiritual "dryness," "darkness," "loneliness," and "torture"—feelings she compared to the experience of hell—to the point of causing her to doubt the existence of heaven and even of God Himself.[9]

She acknowledged being acutely aware of the discrepancy between her inner state and her public demeanor. She even stated that her smile was a mask that covered everything. Despite her religious fervor and selfless love to the needy in Calcutta, she lamented over her experience of spiritual darkness and emptiness:

> Lord, my God, who am I that you should forsake me? The Child of your Love—and now become as the most hated one—the one—You have thrown away as unwanted—unloved. I call, I cling, I want—and there is no One to answer, no One on Whom I can cling—no, No One.—Alone ... Where is my Faith even deep down right in there is nothing, but emptiness and darkness—My God—how painful is this unknown pain—I have no Faith—I dare not utter the words and thoughts that crowd in my heart—and make me suffer untold agony. So many unanswered questions live within me afraid to uncover them—because of the blasphemy—If there be a God—please forgive me. When I try to raise my thoughts to Heaven—there is such convicting emptiness that those very thoughts return like sharp knives and hurt my very soul. I am told God loves me, and yet the reality of darkness and coldness and emptiness is so great that nothing touches my soul. Did I make a mistake in surrendering blindly to the Call of the Sacred Heart?[10]

How incredibly sad! Notwithstanding the false gospel of salvation by works that she embraced as a Roman Catholic, like so many, she was religious, and even suffered for Christ, but not the *true* Christ. She therefore knew nothing of the love and joy of a Christ she could feel and sense consistent with the testimony of Scripture and those who are truly united to Him in genuine saving faith. She knew nothing of what it is to be the object of the Father's delight, even as Christ, in whom every true believer exists (John 17:26). She knew nothing of the living hope that animates the redeemed to "greatly rejoice, even though now for a little while, if necessary, you have been distressed by various trials, that the proof of your faith . . . even though tested by fire, may be found to result in praise and glory and honor at the revelation of Jesus Christ" (1 Peter 1:6-7).

It is tragic to consider how radically different Mother Teresa's testimony is from the testimony of those who have truly been "justified by faith" and "have peace with God through our Lord Jesus Christ" (Rom. 5:1); who therefore "exult in . . . tribulations, knowing that tribulation brings about perseverance; and perseverance, proven character; and proven character, hope; and hope does not disappoint, because the love of God has been poured out within our hearts through the Holy Spirit who was given to us" (Rom 5:3-5). This is such an astounding reality, a testimony to the immensity of God's grace. Because the indwelling Spirit is the "earnest of our inheritance" (Eph. 1:14), it is He who generates a felt joy of God's love for us as part of our earthly inheritance, a foretaste of the day when Christ's bridal church will be brought to her Groom for the final consummation of her promised espousal.

But as we yearn for that day during this season of our betrothal, the Spirit makes us wonderfully aware of the intimacy we currently enjoy because of the indwelling Christ (1 John 4:13). Was this not the magnificent tenor of His yearning on our behalf when He petitioned the Father asking "that the love with which You loved Me may be in them, and I in them" (John 17:26)? Indeed it was; and it is right now! Because of this, we are able to say with the psalmist, "God my exceeding joy" (Ps. 43:4).

Tares Among the Wheat

But sadly, all this is quite foreign to the experience of many "Christless" Christians, though they seldom admit it, until their formalism and hypocrisy betray them. Most of us have had friends and even family members who claimed to love Christ and appeared to be His faithful servants, but then to our dismay we gradually see the emergence of a person we never really knew. The orthodox Christian doctrines they once claimed become twisted, ignored, or jettisoned completely. Their lifestyle that once bore some semblance of the righteousness of Christ now displays the unrighteousness of those who hate Him. Instead of manifesting the abiding results of the new life in Christ where "the old things passed away" and "behold, new things have come" (2 Cor. 5:17), their character and conduct prove they are still alienated from God, "because the mind set on the flesh is hostile toward God; for it does not subject itself to the law of God, for it is not even able to do so; and those who are in the flesh cannot please God" (Rom. 8:7). As a pastor, I have encountered this sad phenomenon more times than I can count.

But what we must bear in mind is that the bad seed that produces spiritual defection grows slowly and secretly over time before its worthless fruit becomes evident. As Jesus said in his parable of the wheat and tares, He sows the good seeds and the devil sows the bad seeds, mingling his children with God's; *but it is impossible to discern the true from the false, until the head matures at harvest—and that takes time* (Matt. 13:24-30, 36-43).

Paul also warned about this dangerous phenomenon in the context of choosing qualified pastors/elders saying, "The sins of some men are quite evident, going before them to judgment; for others, their sins follow after" (1 Tim. 5:24). And we've all been witnesses to this. The sins of some are so obvious it is easy to make an early judgment, but for others, the test of time is necessary to reveal a man's true character.

But when it comes to distinguishing true from false believers, the stakes are much higher. It's one thing to be disqualified from pastoral ministry, but it's infinitely more serious to be disqualified from entrance into the kingdom of heaven—which will be the fate of most so-called "Christians" who call Jesus "Lord" (Matt. 7:13-23) but who do not submit to His lordship (Luke 6:46). He made this abundantly clear in His terrifying warning against those who are Christian in name only when He said,

> Not everyone who says to Me, "Lord, Lord," will enter the kingdom of heaven, but he who does the will of My Father who is in heaven *will enter*. Many will say to Me on that day, "Lord, Lord, did we not prophesy in Your name, and in Your name cast out demons, and in Your name perform many miracles?" And then I will declare to them, "I never knew you;

depart from Me, you who practice lawlessness."
(Matt. 7:21-23)

The Transforming Power of Regeneration

Indeed, *truth and time walk hand in hand*, and this will also be true of genuine saving faith—the product of regeneration whereby we are joined to the Lord and made to be "one spirit *with Him*" (1 Cor. 6:16; *cf.* John 3:9; Eph. 2:10). The genuine expression of saving and sanctifying grace will become increasingly obvious over time in the life of one who has truly been born again—a marvelous transformation to behold. True saving faith is obedient faith. It is the living manifestation of the good work that Christ began in us and has promised to perfect (Phil. 1:6). It is living proof that God has miraculously given us a radically new nature that changes not only our *behaviors*, but our *desires* (1 Cor. 6:11; 2 Cor. 5:17), making our "ambition . . . to be pleasing to Him" (v. 9), and empowering us to "cleanse ourselves from all defilement of flesh and spirit, perfecting holiness in the fear of God" (7:1).

When Christ Himself becomes our very life, our character and conduct will increasingly bear the fruit of His righteous affections, desires, longings, virtues, and behaviors. As a result, when others accurately assess the life of one who has truly been born again, they will give testimony to a progressive, measurable transformation into the likeness of Christ—thus proving the reality of this vital and indissoluble union.

What an astounding thought: that He is *in* us and we are *in* Him! Because we are united to Christ in His death, burial, and resurrection, our old self has been "crucified with him" (Rom. 6:6; *cf.* Gal. 2:20). Even as Christ's death was followed by resurrection, our death to sin and our baptism into his death result in a resurrection to new life in Christ. Paul summarized these amazing parallels saying that

> we have been buried with Him through baptism into death, so that as Christ was raised from the dead through the glory of the Father, so we too might walk in newness of life. For if we have become united with Him in the likeness of His death, certainly we shall also be in the likeness of His resurrection, knowing this, that our old self was crucified with Him, in order that our body of sin might be done away with, so that we would no longer be slaves to sin; for he who has died is freed from sin. (Rom. 6:4-7)

This speaks of the power of regeneration that produces a radically new life principle, a new disposition, a new quality and character to our lives controlled by a new nature (*cf.* Ezek. 36:26; 2 Cor. 5:17; Gal. 6:15; Eph. 4:24).

Because we are united to Christ we have been made "partakers of the divine nature, having escaped the corruption that is in the world by lust" (2 Peter 1:4). Every true believer has been "born of [God]" (1 John 2:29) making personal holiness the ruling conviction and aspiration of his life. The new birth is a miraculous work of the Spirit (John 3:5, 6,8; 6:63; Titus 3:5; *cf.* Rom 8:2; 2 Cor. 3:6) whereby He plants the divine "seed" of life into the heart of a newborn soul causing that man or woman to be repulsed by that which God abhors. Therefore, "No one born of God makes a practice of sinning, for God's seed abides in him, and he cannot keep on sinning because he has been born of God" (1 John 3:9), causing one to say, "His commandments are not burdensome" (1 John 5:3), "I delight to do your will, O my God; Your law is within my heart" (Ps. 40:8).

Though the principle of sin remains in our unredeemed flesh (Rom. 7:14-25), we are no longer slaves to it (Rom. 6:22), and by the power of the indwelling Spirit we are able to wage war against it and put it to death (8:12-13). Every believer can attest to this in varying measure in his or her life. Though the application of redemption begins at regeneration, it is applied throughout our lives in the process of sanctification whereby the Spirit transforms us into the likeness of Christ over time (2 Cor. 3:18) as He empowers us to gain victory over sin and to manifest the fruits of righteousness (Rom. 6:13). As the Spirit indwells (1 Cor. 3:16), He fills or controls the obedient believer (Eph. 5:18), He produces spiritual fruit in our life (Gal. 5:22-23), and gifts us for service in the church (1 Cor. 12:4) that we might put the holiness, power, and glory of Christ on display.

The Steady Descent into Worldliness

Yet anyone who is willing to make an honest evaluation will agree that the dominating mark of contemporary evangelicalism is one of increasing *worldliness*, not *holiness*—certain proof that regeneration has never taken place. Sin has been so redefined that virtually no one should feel guilty about anything. Moreover, hardened resistance and opposition to even the clearest teachings of Scripture is now gaining momentum as thousands of professing Christians jump on the train of cultural acceptance. The approval of homosexual immorality and transgenderism—both of which contradict God's holy purposes in creation and redemption—and the denial of God's design for marriage to be a covenantal union of one man and one woman meant to exemplify the covenant love between Christ and His bridal church are but a few examples among many.

On what basis can a person claim to have been "made . . . alive together with Christ" (Eph. 2:4) when still "(walking) according to the course of this world, according to the prince of the power of the air, of the spirit that is now working in the sons of disobedience" (vv. 2-3)? In this same section of Paul's epistle he reminds those who have truly been made alive in Christ of their pre-Christian life saying, "Among them we too all formerly lived in the lusts of our flesh, indulging the desires of the flesh and of the mind, and were by nature children of wrath, even as the rest" (v. 3). Yet much of the church today embraces Satan's world system by promoting the values and standards that are blatantly offensive to God. A cursory perusal of the unbiblical "spiritual" pontifications of many Facebook users betrays the fool's paradise in which most people live. Having no fear of God, their "worldly *and* empty chatter . . . [leads] to further ungodliness, and their talk . . . [spreads] like gangrene" (2 Tim. 2:16).

In 2 Corinthians 10:4-5 Paul refers to Satan's ideologies as spiritual "strongholds," fortresses of demonic deception that can only be destroyed by godly believers who march on their knees in prayer and wield the sword of the Spirit, the Word of God. We must remember that it is only divine truth that can defeat satanic deceptions (Eph. 6:17-18; *cf.* Heb. 4:12) and set people free from them so they can be brought captive to the truth and obedience to Christ.

I frequently talk with people who are leaving their churches because, as one godly man put it, "My church has become the satanic fortress of 2 Corinthians 10!" But what is really frightening in this regard is the inescapable clarity of Scripture that defines those who disregard and disobey the will of the Father as *those who are self-deceived and will not enter the kingdom regardless of their profession to the contrary* (Matt. 7:21). Genuine discipleship is always determined by the fruit of righteousness one bears on the branch of his or her life as a result of abiding in Christ (John 15:4-5). Jesus said,

> For there is no good tree which produces bad fruit, nor, on the other hand, a bad tree which produces good fruit. For each tree is known by its own fruit. For men do not gather figs from thorns, nor do they pick grapes from a briar bush. The good man out of the good treasure

of his heart brings forth what is good; and the evil man out of the evil treasure brings forth what is evil; for his mouth speaks from that which fills his heart.
(Luke 6:43-45)

No matter how religious a person claims to be, if he or she scoffs at the clear teaching of Scripture by embracing false doctrine and living in blatant disobedience to the will of God, that person has never been united to Christ in saving faith, and has no love for the truth or for Christ as characterized in Paul's prayer for the saints in Philippi:

And this I pray, that your love may abound still more and more in real knowledge and all discernment, so that you may approve the things that are excellent, in order to be sincere and blameless until the day of Christ; having been filled with the fruit of righteousness which comes through Jesus Christ, to the glory and praise of God.
(Phil. 1:9-11).

Unfortunately, the new birth as a supernatural work of God known only by its results has been replaced by a false gospel that allows anyone who says he or she loves God to be considered "born again" and heaven bound. You see this at funerals all the time where the deceased is said to be "in a better place" despite the obvious lack of love for Christ and passion for His glory that marked that person's life.

Rejecting Truth, Enslaved by Myths

It is shocking to see the alarming rise of those within the ranks of evangelicalism who have no fear of God, no fear of judgment, and no respect for God's Word. Paul warned Timothy of this very thing in the first century when he said,

> For the time will come when they will not endure sound doctrine; but *wanting* to have their ears tickled, they will accumulate for themselves teachers in accordance to their own desires, and will turn away their ears from the truth and will turn aside to myths.
> (2 Tim. 4:3-4)

While examples of this abound, one in particular stands out. A colleague directed my attention to an ad for a Teaching Pastor position on an online church staffing website. It read as follows:

CATEGORIES: Teaching Pastor
DENOMINATIONS: Non-Denominational
CHURCH SIZE: 751 to 1000
JOB TYPE: Full-Time

JOB DESCRIPTION:
They will be open-minded and non-religious. They will have a solid grasp of the principles and values that Jesus taught. They will avoid bringing politics or activism to the platform. They will have excellent speaking skills. They will have the ability to complete a message in a timely fashion and the ability to deliver it in the 30 minutes or less time allowance.

(Name of church) is in agreement with Rob Bell, John Shelby Spong, and other more liberal leaders. We are an all-inclusive community that welcomes and affirms all, regardless of history or sexual orientation or preference.

Our goal as a community church is not to get people "saved", as they do not need saving. We believe in the transformative power of love and grace that Jesus offers, but do not believe in traditional punitive models of hell requiring salvation. Our founding pastor is a theologian and has a Ph.D. concentrating in Biblical Critical Methodologies.

Responsibilities include but are not limited to:

- Writing, preparing, and delivering the weekend message as needed. We currently offer three weekend services (same message each time).
- Working with other members of the teaching staff to develop series themes.
- Providing pastoral service for funerals and weddings as needed.
- Attending all weekend services and other functions to socialize with the community.
- Pastoral visits to hospice and other medical facilities as needed.
- Contribute as needed in our podcast and church blog.

This is a full-time salaried position, open immediately.[11]

What is even more appalling than the proud apostasy stated in this solicitation is the reality that this example is representative of what is now becoming the rule rather than the exception among churches. To be sure, most so-called "Christians" are indistinguishable from non-Christians. Instead of confronting the world, the church has become the world

(Rom. 12:2). Instead of coming out of the world and being separated from it (2 Cor. 6:14-18), many professing evangelicals have fallen more in love with it, proving they are enemies of God (James 4:4), indifferent to the Spirit's warning:

> Do not love the world, nor the things in the world. If anyone loves the world, the love of the Father is not in him. For all that is in the world, the lust of the flesh and the lust of the eyes and the boastful pride of life, is not from the Father, but is from the world. And the world is passing away, and also its lusts; but the one who does the will of God abides forever.
> (1 John 2:15-17)

Responding to this kind of lamentable lip service to the Lordship of Christ Jesus asked, "Why do you call Me, 'Lord, Lord,' and do not do what I say" (Luke 6:46)? The answer is obvious: He is *not* their Lord and they do not belong to Him. Jesus said, "My sheep hear My voice, and I know them, and they follow Me" (John 10:27).

While none of us is perfect, the mark of authentic Christianity will be the imitation of Christ in faith and obedience. This is always the test of true saving faith. Because of our union with Christ, we have been brought into the same fellowship with the Father and the Spirit as He has. Jesus Himself tells us: "If anyone loves Me, he will keep My word; and My Father will love him, and We will come to him and make Our abode with him. He who does not love Me does not keep My words" (John 14:23-24a). James describes those who are united to Christ this way:

> By this we know that we have come to know Him, if we keep His commandments. The one who says, "I have come to know Him," and does not keep His commandments, is a liar, and the truth is not in him; but whoever keeps His word, in him the love of God has truly been perfected. By this we know that we are in Him: the one who says he abides in Him ought himself to walk in the same manner as He walked.
> (1 John 2:3-6)

A Temple of the Living God

It cannot be clearer: *the fruit of authentic regeneration and union with Christ is a life of joyful and habitual obedience motivated by a sincere love for Christ.* And it is this visible proof that constitutes an *objective* assurance of our salvation while at the same time confirming the *subjective*, internal witness of the Holy Spirit (1 John 5:10; Rom. 8:14-16; 2 Cor. 1:12). Furthermore—and this is incomprehensible—because of our union with Christ we are also united to the Father and the Holy Spirit as He is (John 10:30). Indeed, "we are a temple of the living God" (2 Cor. 6:16), "[we] are built together into a dwelling of God in the Spirit" (Eph. 2:22), our "life is hidden with Christ in God" (Col. 3:3). And because of this Jesus says, "If anyone loves Me, he will keep My word; and My Father will love him, and We will come to him and make Our abode with him" (John 14:23).

The implications of this ineffable union as they relate to life and godliness cannot be overemphasized. That the Triune Godhead dwells within the redeemed explains the God-exalting disposition and supernatural resources they possess to cause them to bear the fruit of righteousness for the glory of God. This, of course, is in contrast to the apostate Christian who is only superficially attached to the vine—Christ—and is therefore a non-fruit-bearing branch that must be removed and burned, a subject we will now examine in chapter four.

4

The Vine and the Branches

"Abide in Me, and I in you. As the branch cannot bear fruit of itself unless it abides in the vine, so neither can you unless you abide in Me. . . . If anyone does not abide in Me, he is thrown away as a branch and dries up; and they gather them, and cast them into the fire and they are burned.
JOHN 15:4, 6

It was Thursday night of the Passion Week of Christ, the eve of His crucifixion. Jesus, along with his twelve disciples, celebrated the Feast of Passover in the customary manner of Judaism. But the disciples did not realize two very important things that Jesus knew: one, that He was transforming that meal into a memorial that pictured Himself as the Lamb of God, the ultimate Passover sacrifice (John 1:29; 1 Cor. 5:7); and two, that a traitor was among them. Both realities would require instruction on Jesus' part, but I only wish to deal with the matter of Judas for the sake of our discussion.

While we all try to be discerning, it is impossible to truly know a person's heart. As we have discussed earlier, just because a person claims to be a Christian doesn't mean he is one. Judas was a perfect example. He had everyone duped, except the Lord who knew his heart all along. Even after Jesus said that His betrayer would be the one "whom I shall give a piece of bread when I have dipped it . . . then gave it to Judas" (John 13:26) — resulting in his departure — *still* "no one at the table knew for what reason He said this to him" (v. 28). The eleven remaining disciples remained clueless. Moreover, because Jesus so easily passed the morsel of betrayal to Judas, it is highly probable that he was seated near the Lord in a position of honor during that final Passover meal.

You have to wonder if even Judas himself believed he truly loved Christ. Can anyone be that self-deceived? I believe the answer is, "Yes, absolutely!" When Jesus announced to his disciples that one of them would betray Him, even "Judas, who was betraying Him, answered and said, 'Rabbi, is it I?' [Jesus] said to him, 'You have said it'" (Matt. 26:25).

What Is a Christian?

So the question we must ask is simply this: *What is a Christian?* Or to put it differently, *What validates genuine saving faith?* While the answer to this query is multi-faceted, at a most fundamental level it is rooted in the concept of a believer's union with Christ. While numerous passages attest to this truth (as we have already discussed), Jesus' words recorded in John 15:4-5 provide an excellent summary:

> Abide in Me, and I in you. As the branch cannot bear fruit of itself unless it abides in the vine, so neither can you unless you abide in Me. I am the vine, you are the branches; he who abides in Me and I in him, he bears much fruit, for apart from Me you can do nothing.

In light of a believer's union with Christ, we can answer the question "what is a Christian?" as follows: A *Christian is one in whom the Triune Godhead dwells eternally, empowering that individual to manifest the fruit of His righteousness for His glory.* This was obviously missing in the life of Judas, but it was impossible to detect until his faith was tested. None of his closest companions had any reason to be suspicious of Judas. There was nothing about his testimony or service to Christ that would indicate his secret goal to cash in on the kingdom; nothing to suggest that he merely saw Jesus as his ticket to personal prosperity; nothing to show he had no love of the truth and certainly no love for Christ. No one could detect his progressive bitterness and disillusionment with Christ. Nothing exposed his hypocrisy; he kept it well hidden from everyone except Jesus who was deeply "troubled in spirit" (John 13:21).

And how absurd it is to see how Judas feared man more than God Himself! After Jesus sent him away to complete his cowardly conspiracy, Judas agreed with the chief priests and captains about the price of his betrayal, and then he began "seeking a good opportunity to betray Him to them apart from the multitude" (Luke 22:6). What a testimony to the insanity of depravity!

But hypocrisy is as deadly as it is deceptive. Judas' kiss of betrayal exposed the evil of feigned love and his subsequent gruesome suicide revealed the fatal consequence of pretense, causing Jesus to say of him, "It would have been good for that man if he had never been born" (Mark 14:21). Like countless others, Judas was a living example of the deceptive faithlessness and fruitlessness of hypocrisy.

We would all do well to examine our heart in light of these truths and say with the psalmist, "Search me, O God, and know my heart" (Ps. 139:23)—not to provoke fear and doubt, but to affirm sincerity, confidence, and peace, that from a pure heart we might render praise to the One who purchased our redemption with His very blood. But if our examination uncovers insincerity and secret strategies of hypocrisy, every effort must be made to get right with God who says, "I, the Lord, search the heart, I test the mind, even to give to each man according to his ways, according to the results of his deeds" (Jer. 17:10).

Jesus—The True Vine

After Satan had filled Judas and he had departed to betray Jesus, the gospel record reveals that our Lord announced His departure, predicted Peter's denial, comforted His disciples by promising His return, emphasized the need for the habitual practice of obedience to His commands as proof of the believer's love for him and the Father, and promised that the Father would send the Holy Spirit in His name. Then He instructed the remaining eleven disciples through the use of an extended metaphor of a vine and its branches recorded in John 15:1-11—a lesson that vividly distinguishes true from false Christians. This was crucial for their understanding, because they were about to see one of their own betray their precious Master.

Jesus begins by saying, "I am the true vine" (v. 1). This is the last of the "I am" (Greek *ego eimi*) declarations where Jesus asserts His deity and his saving relationship toward the world. The title, "I am" bears the Old Testament divine name of Yahweh, the same title of deity disclosed to Moses at the burning bush in Exodus 3:14. Previously in John 8 Jesus infuriated the Pharisees by declaring Himself to be Yahweh, the Lord of the Old Testament, when He said to them, "Truly, truly, I say to you, before Abraham was born, I am" (v. 58). This was also the infinitely powerful declaration of Himself that caused the soldiers, officers, and Judas himself to fall helplessly to the ground when they came to arrest Him (John 18:6).

That Jesus claimed to be Yahweh, "the true vine," was of utmost importance, because in the Old Testament the vine symbolized Israel, the covenant people of God (Ps. 80:9-16; Is. 5:1-7; 37:2ff; Jer. 2:21; 12:10ff; Ezek. 15:1-8; 17:1-21; 19:10-14; Hos. 10:1-2). But as these references indicate, the vine's failure to produce good fruit was a harbinger of divine judgment upon the nation. It also pointed to the need of a "true vine" that would bring forth good fruit, namely Jesus their Messiah. Throughout Jesus' ministry, He confronted the misplaced trust the Jewish people had in their heritage to save them.

They mistakenly believed that simply because they were born of the seed of Abraham and were therefore people of the covenant they were automatically united to God and the only deserving recipients of His blessing.

But in reality, apart from faith in Jesus their Messiah, "the true vine" (John 1:1) and source of all spiritual blessings and godliness (v. 5), they remained alienated from God, unable to produce the fruit of righteousness that can only flow through Him. While ethnically Abraham is the father of all Jews, he is also the father of both believing Gentiles and Jews who, like him, have been justified through faith alone in Christ alone (Rom. 4); for this reason Abraham is "the father of all those who believe" (v. 11) and "the father" of those "who walk in the steps of the faith" (v. 12). Jesus is the "High Priest" and "Minister of the sanctuary and of the true tabernacle which the Lord erected, and not man" (Heb. 8:1-2), the "Mediator of a better covenant, which was established on better promises" (v. 6); a reference to the "new covenant" (vv. 8, 13; 9:15) that is *internal* in contrast to the Covenant of Law that was primarily *external* (Heb 8:10; *cf.* Ezek. 36:26, 27).

Jesus wanted his disciples to understand that only those connected to the "true vine" by genuine saving faith (unlike many in Israel, and unlike Judas) were the recipients of divine blessing, validated by their fruit of righteousness (John 15:4). He made the same assertion earlier in John 14:6 when He said, "I am the way, and the truth, and the life; no one comes to the Father but through Me." So when Jesus said, "I am the true vine" (v. 1), He was not only asserting His deity ("I am") but also, because He is the "true vine," He was the perfect, genuine, complete, and essential vine, in contradistinction to the vine of Israel that "he expected . . . to produce good grapes, but it produced only worthless ones" (Isaiah 5:2). Judas was a living illustration of just that.

Like so many over the course of redemptive history, including our modern era, many people have a superficial attachment to Jesus due to a meaningless, insincere profession of faith or a mere church affiliation. "Nevertheless," as Carson aptly states, "by failing to display the grace of perseverance (they) finally testify that the transforming life of Christ has never pulsated within them (*e.g.* Mt. 13:18–23; 24:12; Jn. 8:31ff; Heb. 3:14–19; 1 Jn. 2:19; 2 Jn. 9).[12] The disciples had to learn, like all of us, that Israel was the *type*, but Christ is the superior *antitype* that bears the righteous fruit that satisfies all the expectations of the vinedresser, who is the "Father" (v. 1b). No one can bear spiritual fruit apart from abiding in the vine of Christ Jesus. Where there is an absence of the fruit of righteousness and persevering faith, there is no spiritual connection and no spiritual life.

The Father—the Vinedresser

Indeed, as Jesus states, "My Father is the vinedresser" (v. 1b). He is the husbandman who cares for the Vine. It was the Father's tender love for His Son who guarded Him as a child when He "grew up before Him like a tender shoot, and like a root out of parched ground" (Isa. 53:2). But Jesus goes on to explain how the divine husbandman is now occupied with two primary tasks; one, *he must remove branches that bear no fruit*; and two, *he must prune branches that do, so they will bear more fruit*. The distinction between these two kinds of branches was crucial for the disciples' understanding, which Jesus goes on to describe, "Every branch in Me that does not bear fruit, He takes away; and every *branch* that bears fruit, He prunes it so that it may bear more fruit" (v. 2). These two distinctly different branches symbolize the two kinds of disciples that outwardly profess faith in Christ: the true, fruit-bearing branches that abide in Him, versus the false, non-fruit-bearing branches that do not abide in Him.

This is not, as some will argue, a reference to two different kinds of Christians: true believers who bear fruit versus true believers who sin and lose their salvation or who fail to bear any fruit. (I've even heard some say that God will remove those who don't bear enough fruit—implying the heresy of salvation by works.) No "true believer" loses his salvation or abandons the faith. The unified testimony of Scripture refutes such a notion. The believer's security is anchored in the unchanging love, omnipotent power, and sovereign will of the Father who set His love upon His elect in eternity past and granted them grace in Christ Jesus (2 Tim. 1:9). The merits of Christ's atoning work on the cross and the efficacy of His present intercession secure the salvation of all who have been united to Him (Rom. 8:33-39), along with the sealing ministry of the Holy Spirit (Eph. 1:13-14; *cf.* 4:30).

Furthermore, there's no such thing as a "fruitless" Christian. A "fruitless" Christian is no Christian at all, like Judas Iscariot. This is Jesus' point. Those who "abide in Him" (John 15:7) will "bear much fruit, and *so* prove to be My disciples" (v. 8); they will be the ones, as Jesus says, who will "keep My commandments . . . abide in My love, just as I have kept My Father's commandments and abide in His love" (v. 10). All true Christians will bear *some fruit* because they are supernaturally attached to the vine. Paul says, "by His doing you are in

Christ Jesus, who became to us wisdom from God, and righteousness and sanctification, and redemption" (1 Cor. 1:30). Because every true disciple has been "crucified with Christ" (Gal. 2:20), "died with Christ" (Col. 2:20), "buried with Him" (Rom. 6:4), "raised up together . . . in Christ" (Eph. 2:6), "seated together in heavenly places in Christ" (Eph. 2:6), and "hid with Christ in God" (Col. 3:3), the life-giving power of the Lover of our soul nourishes every branch, causing it to produce more likeness to Him in character and conduct.

Fruit in Keeping with Repentance

John the Baptist challenged his hearers to "bear fruit in keeping with repentance" (Matt. 3:8), then went on to warn, "every tree that does not bear good fruit is cut down and thrown into the fire" (v. 10). Judas Iscariot is the most visible example of this. In His parable of the sower (Matt. 13:18-23), Jesus described the *superficial hearers* who attend our churches today: "This is the man who hears the word, and immediately receives it with joy; yet he has no firm root in himself, but is only temporary, and when affliction or persecution arises because of the word, immediately he falls away" (vv. 20-21). He went on to describe *worldly hearers*, "the one on whom seed was sown among the thorns, this is the man who hears the word, and the worry of the world, and the deceitfulness of riches choke the word, and it becomes unfruitful" (v. 22). Then finally, in His concluding parable of the wheat and the tares (vv. 24-43), He described how hard it can be to distinguish between true and false disciples, because "both . . . grow together until the harvest," at which time "[He] will say to the reapers, 'First gather up the tares and bind them in bundles to burn them up; but gather the wheat into my barn'" (v. 30).

There have always been and there will always be *false professors* who attach themselves to the church, but not to Christ. This is pandemic in the *institutional church* of Christian liberalism (which is thoroughly apostate), and it makes up the majority of the *cultural church* that dominates the evangelical church today. Plants produce fruit consistent with their nature, according to the genetic information stored in the DNA molecules that provide the instruction used in the development and function of all known live organisms. The same is true spiritually. Just as plants produce fruit in keeping with their nature, people will do the same. True believers have been made "partakers of the divine nature" (2 Peter 1:4) and will therefore manifest characteristics in keeping with their divine nature. Phony believers will manifest characteristics in keeping with their fallen nature, like the ultra-religious Pharisees of whom Jesus said, "You are of your father the devil, and you want to do the desires of your father.... Whenever he speaks a lie, he speaks from his own *nature*; for he is a liar, and the father of lies" (John 8:44).

Since all true disciples will bear some fruit, Jesus is not referring to Christians who don't bear fruit, but to those who profess Christ in name only, "Christless" Christians who cannot bear fruit in keeping with repentance. Grapes will not grow on thistles! Jesus made this clear when He said, "There is no good tree which produces bad fruit, nor, on the other hand, a bad tree which produces good fruit" (Luke 6:43; *cf.* Matt. 7:17-20). Moreover, this does not refer to believers who lose their salvation. Jesus promised He would not forcibly remove any true disciples: "All that the Father gives Me will come to Me, and the one who comes to Me I will certainly not cast out" (John 6:37). It is obvious in Jesus' extended metaphor of the vine and the branches that only dead branches that bear no fruit are thrown away and burned—a judgment motif that extends beyond the Old Testament judgments against Israel, and even beyond the immediate implication of Judas Iscariot, but includes all fruitless branches superficially attached to Jesus through some form of external religious affiliation but not through a vital (living) union by which Christ's life becomes one with those who are in Him (Gal. 2:20; Col. 3:3-4).

Characteristics of Branches that Abide in the Vine

The imagery our Lord provides is a powerful reminder of the mutual indwelling of Christ and His own and the fruitful harvest such an intimate union will produce. There are six prominent characteristics of true branches united to Christ that emerge from His extended metaphor, each providing both comforting assurance and spiritual discernment to those who truly belong to Christ.

First, *all true believers bear spiritual fruit, unlike false disciples who do not and cannot bear spiritual fruit.* As part of this chosen vine, genuine disciples will manifest the fruit in keeping with the source of their life. They will look like Christ! Doing the will of the Father will be the passion and pattern of their life and they will obey the Word of Christ: "If you continue in My word, then you are truly disciples of Mine" (John 8:31). You don't see any concern for these matters in a false disciple, though he may attend a church, or even be pastor of a church.

Basically, all behavior that is God-honoring will be the fruit of this vine—"fruit in keeping with repentance" (Matt. 3:8)—what Paul called the "fruit of righteousness which comes through Jesus Christ, to the glory and praise of God" (Phil. 1:11). Spiritual fruit includes virtues like the fruit of the Spirit: "love, joy, peace, patience, kindness, goodness, faithfulness, gentleness, self-control" (Gal. 5:22).

- *Love* is the love of choice that manifests itself to joyful, sacrificial service.
- *Joy* refers to that soul-satisfying happiness anchored in a faith that is confident God is at work in us for our good and His glory, regardless of circumstances.
- *Peace* is an inner tranquility, come what may, which results from confidence in one's saving relationship with Christ.
- *Patience* speaks of one's ability to endure injuries inflicted by others and the willingness to accept them.
- *Kindness* speaks of treating others with the same tenderness as the Lord treats all believers.
- *Goodness* refers to moral and spiritual excellence manifested in active kindness.
- *Faithfulness* is loyalty and trustworthiness.
- *Gentleness* (meekness) refers to patient humility

that causes one to endure every offense with no desire for revenge or retribution. The term is used in the New Testament to speak of submission to the will of God, a heart that is teachable and considerate of others.
- *Self-control* refers to the Spirit-empowered ability to restrain passions and appetites.

Every genuine disciple of Christ is a branch attached to the Vine that is Christ, and each branch is a conduit through which the fruit-producing spiritual molecules will flow to produce these magnificent clusters of God-honoring fruit.

SECOND, *not only do true disciples bear fruit, but they abide in Christ's love*. Jesus said, "Just as the Father has loved Me, I have also loved you; abide in My love. If you keep My commandments, you will abide in My love; just as I have kept My Father's commandments and abide in His love" (vv. 9-10). "Abide in my love" is a phrase Jesus uses repeatedly in this metaphor meaning to remain or continue—the obvious result of being united to Christ as Jesus declared, ". . .you in me, and I in you" (14:20).

However, it is important not to confuse being *"in Christ"* with *"abiding in Christ."* We are *"in Christ"* permanently as a result of the union effected by

God. But we are exhorted to *"abide in Christ,"* meaning we are to remain in fellowship with God in Christ—to have a sustained conscious communion with Him—because sometimes that fellowship is interrupted by sin. So to be "in Christ" is a matter of *grace*; to "abide in Him" is a matter of *responsibility*.

Paul exhorted the Ephesians in this regard saying, "Do not be foolish, but understand what the will of the Lord is. And do not get drunk with wine . . . but be filled with the Spirit" (Eph. 5:15-16). John MacArthur is helpful in his remarks on this important concept:

> True communion with God is not induced by drunkenness, but by the Holy Spirit. Paul is not speaking of the Holy Spirit's indwelling (Rom. 8:9) or the baptism by Christ with the Holy Spirit (1 Cor. 12:12:13), because every Christian is indwelt and baptized by the Spirit at the time of salvation. He is rather giving a command for believers to live continually under the influence of the Spirit by letting the Word control them (Col. 3:16), pursuing pure lives, confessing all known sin, dying to self, surrendering to God's will, and depending on His power in all things. Being filled with the Spirit is living in the conscious presence

of the Lord Jesus Christ, letting His mind, through the Word, dominate everything that is thought and done. Being filled with the Spirit is the same as walking in the Spirit (Gal. 5:15-23). Christ exemplified this way of life (Luke 4:1).[13]

Sinful habits like drunkenness (Eph. 5:18) will grieve the Holy Spirit (4:3) and quench Him (1 Thess. 5:19). They will diminish our ability to bear fruit, cause us to forfeit blessing and eternal reward, and subject us to the Father's chastening. If we're not careful, destructive idols can become the preoccupation of our heart rather than Christ.

There will be times in the life of every Christian when we fail to abide in Him, when our love grows cold like the Ephesians who "left [their] first love" (Rev. 2:4), or when in our overconfidence we succumb to temptation like Peter who denied Christ, or when we wittingly or unwittingly yield ourselves to some other form of disobedience. Sadly, some believers seem to never mature and are like the arrogant, worldly, divisive saints in Corinth (1 Cor. 3:1-3) who were notorious for yielding to the passions of their fallen flesh and the pressures of the world that required much patience and loving exhortation on the part of the apostle Paul.

How sad to witness so many churches today cater to these very people by offering them a country club environment that promotes *tolerance* over *truth*, *worldliness* over *holiness*, and *man-centered worship* over *God-centered worship* "in spirit and in truth" (John 4:24). Unfortunately, but not unexpectedly, such misplaced priorities banish believers to an island of spiritual infancy and a life that bears little fruit to glorify the Father. But if indeed they bear *some* fruit—for there is no such thing as a fruitless Christian—they are truly a branch connected to the Vine, and the Father will prune them to make them more productive.

THIRD, *the Father will prune spiritually unproductive branches.* Jesus went on to say, "Every *branch* that bears fruit, He prunes it so that it may bear more fruit. You are already clean because of the word which I have spoken to you" (vv. 2b-3). Like every good husbandman, the Father will cut away those things that restrict our ability to bear fruit, that weaken our spiritual immune system, that inhibit our growth—and Scripture will be His pruning sheers. This is why it is so important to be consistently exposed to accurate biblical teaching. The Father is ever vigilant to make us more productive, and He will use the sanctifying truths of His Word

(John 17:17) in concert with the circumstances of our life (Rom. 8:28) and His loving discipline (Heb. 12:7-11; *cf.* 1 Cor. 11:32) to make us bear more fruit for His glory and our joy. The Father's "pruning involves cutting away anything that limits righteousness, including the discipline that comes from trials, suffering, and persecution. The knowledge that the Father uses the pain that Christians endure for their ultimate good should eliminate all fear, self-pity, and complaining."[14]

FOURTH, *they will be blessed by answered prayer.* Jesus goes on to make this amazing promise, "If you abide in Me, and My words abide in you, ask whatever you wish, and it will be done for you" (v. 7). But notice the three conditions for answered prayer. First, *He only answers the prayers of those who abide in Him, who are united to Christ through repentant faith.* Unless it accomplishes His sovereign purposes, God is not obligated to answer the prayers of unbelievers. Second, *prayers must be offered in Jesus' name,* as Jesus stated earlier in chapter 14, "Whatever you ask in My name, that will I do, so that the Father may be glorified in the Son. If you ask Me anything in My name, I will do it" (vv. 13-14). This means that our prayers must be in harmony with God's revealed will in Scripture and His Kingdom purposes. For this reason Jesus asks us to pray, "Your kingdom come, Your will be done, on earth as it is in heaven" (Matt. 6:10).

Furthermore, we must approach God on the merits of Christ alone, acknowledging our utter dependence upon Him and expressing a sincere desire that God be glorified in His answer, that in all things Christ might have the preeminence.

And finally, *prayers must be offered by those in which Christ's "words abide"*; those who decisively commit themselves to the specific words of Christ, whose lives are controlled by the Word and will of God, not the sinful passions of the flesh and the allurements of the world. It stands to reason that those who abide in Christ and are controlled by His words will ask nothing that is contrary to the will of Christ, and therefore receive whatever they ask.

FIFTH, *they will have the privilege of living lives that glorify God and thus validate the genuineness of their faith.* Jesus said, "My Father is glorified by this, that you bear much fruit, and *so* prove to be My disciples" (v. 8). Fruit bearing is the essence of genuine discipleship, the result of abiding in Christ. While it is the Spirit that imparts the principle of holiness within us at regeneration and perfects that good work that He began in us, our new nature cannot operate on its own power. It requires a continued work of sanctification, a constant sustaining and continuous renewing, ". . . for apart from Me you can do nothing" (v. 5). And it is our Lord's great desire for us to "bear much fruit" so God can receive great glory. Paul stated it this way, "so that you may approve the things that are excellent, in order to be sincere and blameless until the day of Christ; having been filled with the fruit of righteousness which comes through Jesus Christ, to the glory and praise of God" (Phil. 1:10-11).

As we glorify Christ through our obedience—empowered and directed as result of our living union and communion with Him—we also glorify the Father as He does. The spiritual fruit that adorns the true disciple will reflect the character of Christ to whom we are united, especially when it is bountiful. Like Christ, we glorify the Father through our loving and joyful desire to do His will. As others watch our lives manifest the character of God, they get a small glimpse of who He is, and in this He is glorified and our faith is validated as we show ourselves to be His disciples.

SIXTH, *they will experience the love and joy of intimate fellowship with God*. This would have been so encouraging to the disciples, as it is to all believers, when Jesus said, "Just as the Father has loved Me, I have also loved you; abide in My love. If you keep My commandments, you will abide in My love; just as I have kept My Father's commandments and abide in His love. These things I have spoken to you so that My joy may be in you, and *that* your joy may be made full" (vv. 9-11). This is the soul-satisfying, Spirit-generated, subjective joy of Christ in the consciousness of the abiding believer. This is what animates a "hope [that] does not disappoint, because the love of God poured out within our hearts through the Holy Spirit who was given to us" (Rom. 5:5). Peter described this as "joy inexpressible and full of glory" (1 Peter 1:8), the kind of joy that permeates and controls the life of every obedient believer. Knowing this, Jesus prayed to His Father: "But now I come to You; and these things I speak in the world so that they may have My joy made full in themselves" (John 17:13).

Would that every branch be a live branch that is truly attached *to* the Vine and abides *in* the Vine. Only then can a believer experience and manifest these God-glorifying characteristics which stand in stark contrast to the characteristics of those branches that have never been attached to the Vine through faith.

Characteristics of Branches that Do Not Abide in the Vine

In verse 2 Jesus gives a strong warning, "Every branch in Me that does not bear fruit, He takes away." He goes on to elaborate upon the fate of a fruitless vine saying, "If anyone does not abide in Me, he is thrown away as a branch and dries up; and they gather them, and cast them into the fire and they are burned" (v. 6). In this context, the phrase "in Me" cannot refer to true believers who are united to Christ (because they will always bear fruit and never be taken away). So the Vinedresser (the Father) takes away the branches that have outwardly (superficially) attached themselves to Christ but fail to persevere in the faith. This proves regeneration had never taken place in them, as in the case of Judas Iscariot—the quintessential example of a false (dead) branch.

As I stated earlier, false professors who outwardly resemble true believers will often attach themselves to the church, but not to Christ. However, it is not a man's superficial externals that validate genuine saving faith, but rather it's the Christlike virtues of his heart that produce spiritual fruit. Where the supernatural life in Christ is non-existent, over time the phony Christian will wither away and gradually distance himself or herself from a true New

Testament church and break fellowship with true believers. The truth preached will be too hard to hear and impossible to live. Even unwitting hypocrisy is a hard act to maintain. The joy-filled lives and Christ-exalting perseverance of authentic Christians will slowly frustrate pretenders. They will be like the depraved and doomed apostates Jude described, "men who are hidden reefs in your love feasts when they feast with you without fear, caring for themselves; clouds without water, carried along by winds; autumn trees without fruit, doubly dead, uprooted; wild waves of the sea, casting up their own shame like foam; wandering stars, for whom the black darkness has been reserved forever" (vv. 12-13).

Jesus made it clear that such branches will be "gathered up and cast into the fire and burned" (John 15:6); and in the day of judgment they will protest saying, "Lord, Lord, did we not prophesy in Your name, and You name cast out demons, and in Your name perform many miracles" (Matt. 7:22)? But He will respond with the terrifying sentence, "I never knew you; depart from Me, you who practice lawlessness" (v. 23). What an unspeakable horror awaits those who refuse to truly embrace Christ in genuine brokenness over sin and in repentant faith. Jesus warns that "at the end of the age the angels will come forth and take out the wicked from among the righteous, and will throw them into the furnace of fire; in that place there will be weeping and gnashing of teeth" (Matt. 13:49-50).

Closing Exaltation

No one can fathom the ultimate horror of being separated from Christ. Yet apart from God's grace in saving us, such would be our just punishment. But because of His great mercy, with Paul we can say, "Blessed *be* the God and Father of our Lord Jesus Christ, who has blessed us with every spiritual blessing in the heavenly *places* in Christ, just as He chose us in Him before the foundation of the world, that we would be holy and blameless before Him" (Eph. 1:3).

And I can think of no greater tribute to our union with Christ than that expressed over 300 years ago by the great Oxford theologian, John Owen (1616-1683), and with this we conclude our study of *The Marvel of Being In Christ: Adoring God's Provision of New Life in the Spirit:*

> Our grace of union with Christ, our participation of him and his nature, is our highest exaltation, the greatest and most glorious

grace that we can be made partakers of in this world. He became poor for our sakes, by a participation of our nature, that we through his poverty may be rich in a participation of his, 2 Cor. 8:9. And this is that which gives worth and excellency unto all that we may be afterwards intrusted with. The grace and privileges of believers are very great and excellent, but yet they are such as do belong unto them that are made partakers of Christ, such as are due to the quickening and adorning of all the members of his body; as all privileges of marriage, after marriage contracted, arise from and follow that contract. For being once made co-heirs with Christ, we are made heirs of God, and have a right to the whole inheritance. And, indeed, what greater glory or dignity can a poor sinner be exalted unto, than to be thus intimately and indissolubly united unto the Son of God, the perfection whereof is the glory which we hope and wait for, John 17:22, 23.[15]

Endnotes

1   August Hopkins Strong, *Systematic Theology: A Compendium Designed for the Use of Theological Students, Rev. ed.* (Revell, New York, 1907), 795.

2   Spurgeon sermon: *The Fourfold Treasure*, Sermon #991, delivered April 27, 1871. https://www.spurgeongems.org/vols16-18/chs991.pdf

3   John Calvin, *Institutes of the Christian Religion*, translated by Henry Beveridge (Hendrickson Publishers, Peabody, Massachusetts, 2008), 348-49.

4   John Murray, *Redemption Accomplished and Applied, Reprint* (Eerdmans, Grand Rapids, Michigan, 2015), 161.

5   John MacArthur and Richard Mayhue, General Editors, *Biblical Doctrine: A Systematic Summary of Bible Truth*, (Crossway Wheaton, Illinois, 2017), 603.

6   Sinclair B. Ferguson, *The Whole Christ: Legalism, Antinomianism, and Gospel Assurance—Why the Marrow Controversy Still Matters* (Crossway, Wheaton, Illinois, 2016), 46-47.

7   John Murray, *Redemption Accomplished and Applied*, (Eerdmans, Grand Rapids, Michigan, 1964), 164.

8   http://pewforum.org/2017/08/31/u-s-protestants-are-not-defined-by-reformation-era-controversies-500-years-later/

9   https://time.com/4126238/mother-teresas-crisis-of-faith/

10   Ibid.

11   https://www.churchstaffing.com/job/240812/teaching-pastor/suncoast-community-church/

12   D. A. Carson, *The Gospel according to John* (Leicester,

England; Grand Rapids, MI: Inter-Varsity Press; W.B. Eerdmans, 1991), 515.

13 *The MacArthur Study Bible* (Thomas Nelson, Nashville, Tennessee, 1997), 1812.

14 John F. MacArthur, *John 12-21: The MacArthur New Testament Commentary*, (Chicago: Moody, 1984), 149.

15 John Owen, (1854). *An Exposition of the Epistle to the Hebrews*, (Vol. 21, *The Works of John Owen*) (W. H. Goold, Ed.) (Johnstone and Hunter, Edinburgh, 1849), 149.

CPSIA information can be obtained
at www.ICGtesting.com
Printed in the USA
LVHW081209110420
653044LV00006B/55